37 SEASONS BEFORE THE TORNADO
POEMS

Kraftgriots
Also in the series (POETRY)

David Cook et al: *Rising Voices*
Olu Oguibe: *A Gathering Fear;* winner, 1992 All Africa Okigbo prize for Literature & Honourable mention, 1993 Noma Award for Publishing in Africa
Nnimmo Bassey: *Patriots and Cockroaches*
Okinba Launko: *Dream-Seeker on Divining Chain*
Onookome Okome: *Pendants,* winner, 1993 ANA/Cadbury poetry prize
Nnimmo Bassey: *Poems on the Run*
Ebereonwu: *Suddenly God was Naked*
Tunde Olusunle: *Fingermarks*
Joe Ushie: *Lambs at the Shrine*
Chinyere Okafor: *From Earth's Bedchamber*
Ezenwa-Ohaeto: *The Voice of the Night Masquerade,* joint-winner, 1997 ANA/Cadbury poetry prize
George Ehusani: *Fragments of Truth*
Remi Raji: *A Harvest of Laughters,* joint-winner 1997 ANA/Cadbury poetry prize
Patrick Ebewo: *Self-Portrait & Other Poems*
George Ehusani: *Petals of Truth*
Nnimmo Bassey: *Intercepted*
Joe Ushie: *Eclipse in Rwanda*
Femi Oyebode: *Selected Poems*
Ogaga Ifowodo: *Homeland & Other Poems,* winner, 1993 ANA poetry prize
Godwin Uyi Ojo: *Forlorn Dreams*
Tanure Ojaide: *Delta Blues and Home Songs*
Niyi Osundare: *The Word is an Egg* (2000)
Tayo Olafioye: *A Carnival of Looters* (2000)
Ibiwari Ikiriko: *Oily Tears of the Delta* (2000)
Arnold Udoka: *I am the Woman* (2000)
Akinloye Ojo: *In Flight* (2000)
Joe Ushie: *Hill Songs* (2000)
Ebereonwu: *The Insomniac Dragon* (2000)
Deola Fadipe: *I Make Pondripples* (2000)
Remi Raji: *Webs of Remembrance* (2001)
'Tope Omoniyi: *Farting Presidents and Other Poems* (2001)
Tunde Olusunle: *Rhythm of the Mortar* (2001)
Abdullahi Ismaila: *Ellipsis* (2001)
Tayo Olafioye: *The Parliament of Idiots: Tryst of the Sinators* (2002)
Femi Abodunrin: *It Would Take Time: Conversation with Living Ancestors* (2002)
Nnimmo Bassey: *We Thought It Was Oil But It Was Blood* (2002)
Ebi Yeibo: *A Song For Tomorrow and Other Poems* (2003)
Adebayo Lamikanra: *Heart Sounds* (2003)
Ezenwa-Ohaeto: *The Chants of a Minstrel* (2003), winner, 2004 ANA/NDDC poetry prize and joint-winner, 2005 LNG The Nigeria Prize for Literature
Seyi Adigun: *Kalakini: Songs of Many Colours* (2004)

37 SEASONS BEFORE THE TORNADO
POEMS

Udenta O. Udenta

kraftgriots

Published by
Kraft Books Limited
6A Polytechnic Road, Sango, Ibadan
Box 22084, University of Ibadan Post Office
Ibadan, Oyo State, Nigeria
☏ + 234 (0) 803 348 2474, + 234 (0) 805 129 1191
E-mail: kraftbooks@yahoo.com
www.kraftbookslimited.com

© Udenta O. Udenta, 2015

ISBN 978–978–918–221–3

= KRAFTGRIOTS =
(A literary imprint of Kraft Books Limited)

First published in 1997 by
Fourth Dimension Publishing Co. Ltd.
16th Fifth Avenue, City Layout, P. M. B 01164
Enugu, Nigeria

All rights reserved. No part of this publication may be reproduced, stored in a retrieval system, or transmitted in any form or by any means, electronic, mechanical, photocopying, recording, or otherwise without the prior permission of the copyright holder.

First printing, January 2015

Contents

Preface to the Second Edition 7
Preface 9

BARREN WINDS **13**
Waking 14
Sunset on broken gongs 15
Day and night 16
Wilting 17
The noise is stilled 18
Fire-flies 19
In-between 21
Dark offering 22
Gloom 24
37 seasons before the tornado 25
The third coming 27
Incantations on the third coming 34

DELUGE... .... **35**
Prophecy 36
Season of the deluge 37
Incantations on the deluge 40
Hangmen also die 41
The participant 43
Where will you be? 44
Past and present 46
Troika feast 48
Judgement day 50
Initiation 51
The march of tornado 53
Tornado sequences 58

OTHER VISIONS **61**
Seven kindred spirits 62
Shadows flee at bright light (for V) 64
The truth in my song (for V) 65
A meeting 66
Rupture 68

Preface to the Second Edition

Unlike textbooks, or even works of fiction and drama, it is not often that a collection of poems, lends itself to additional prefatory commentary that may, regrettably, become tendentious. Even in its expansive apprehensible mechanics, and the broad range of themes and idioms that it incarnates, poetry remains a fragile artistic creation, a precious ornament whose authenticity must be forever honoured.

This fragility, contradistinctionally placed in relation to its inner strength, is emblematic of the trembling balance it creates, achieves and then overcomes, between the rhythm of everyday experiences, and its mediation of multi-layered aesthetic categories, diction and meaning with universal significance.

However, this additional note is necessary for a number of reasons. In subsequent readings of the collection since its first publication, I have detected a number of structural errors, as well as typographical and grammatical mistakes (wrong spelling, improper punctuation, problematic tenses, etc,) which I have taken advantage of this second edition to correct. I have also added 10 new poems to the collection, each as a constitutive aesthetic bridge to the earlier effort, with image-imperatives drawn from extant historical and political matters, since Nigeria embarked on a re-democratization process in 1999.

Moreover, for over ten years since the collection was first put out, I doubt if it has attracted but scant commentary or critical analysis, the reason being, in part, its less than wide circulation. Its status as a true work of art is indeterminate, and, thus uncertain. It is only in the context of wide readership and critical exposure that the measure of a creative work's strength or weakness lies. I have embarked on this second effort, genuinely believing that all effort will be made to circulate the collection as widely as possible, not with a view of garnering for it unearned praise but, at least, to alert the ears of those who are connected to our consciousness, share the same experience and inhabit the same atmosphere, about a venture that, after all, may not be worth the labour.

The only peculiar quality of some of the poems in the collection is their prophetic nature; the title poem bears this out. The collection was published early in 1997, though the title poem and the bulk of the other poems in the collection were, indeed, written six or seven years back. Yet, I was able to predict that after 37 years (Seasons) of Nigerian Independence, a rupture will occur in the land whose potency will match the elemental force of a tornado. Indeed, that rupture occurred after the 37th year (1998) with the deaths of Gen. Abacha and Chief M.K.O. Abiola in 1998, their tornado-like effect on the nation, the tumult of a new beginning and the avalanche of hope and despair a cross-eyed democratization agenda unleashed on the land since 1999. The prophetic nature of some of the poems never occurred to me until quite recently, because having written the title poem about 1989 or 1990, little did I know that by the end of 1998, nearly a decade later, it could capture, as creatively as my talent could permit, the essential direction of Nigerian politics.

Udenta O. Udenta
January, 2014.

Preface

Season is another name for year in the same way that wind incarnates geography, turbulence or even quietude. Such contradiction is the joy of poetry, especially the type that deploys allusive and metaphoric sequences for significatory purposes. The celebration of life is the acknowledgement of death just as the arrest of time equally reflects the passage of seasons. Creation has a certain rhythm, as it turns on the axis of experience and reality. Creation is affirmation, not of transcendental knowledge, but of material life nourished by spiritual wealth. These poems affirm life in a process embodying the constant struggle between good and evil, progress and obscurantism, equity and injustice.

Interestingly, the collection is a product of three years (1988 – 1991) of vicarious labour, pursued with vigour, but at times without purpose. Originally written in bits and pieces of paper, on tissue, on inner covers of books and on used envelopes, they echo the quest of a restless mind unwilling to accept defeat. This version is not the only existing one. The other existing manuscript (in long hand) is hopefully, still with my very good friend and soul-mate, Ego Alowes Jimanze. But for my carelessness this collection would long have been published by Ofo Heritage. I have long forgotten what that version looks like, and had rather sought for new meaning from the scraps still with me. Sometimes, whole lines had to be changed (regardless of my earlier objective intention) when it became impossible to read what I wrote in passion, and sometimes, in haste.

The poems need no explanation except that they talk about contemporary reality. Most of them deal with politics and the possibilities of change. Discerning readers would recognize in them, as Jeremy Hawthorn would say, "political events and figures," and when they do the poems will become absurdly simple. It is only then that laughter and pain will ensue.

I owe a lot of debt to those poets I echoed (lovers of poetry will see and hear them in most of the poems) for they provided a lot of inspiration and did come to my aid when my hand, head and imagination faltered. It's all in the light of the Eliotian "Tradition and Individual Talent". He too provided the basis of my creative quest through my re-reading of his notion of "objective correlative".

I salute Dr. Arthur Nwankwo, mentor, teacher and guide, without whose support and encouragement this collection would not have been published. He is truly one of a kind.

To all kindred spirits (provided that this collection is a worthy basis for my initiation), I say welcome to the joy of creation. The same for others, no less gifted and no less enthusiastic.

Udenta O. Udenta
September, 1996

We frequently find that at times when free political and other comment is dangerous, then concealed references to political events and figures become more useful, and are immediately recognized by contemporary readers.
>
> ***Jeremy Hawthorn***
> ***(Unlocking The Text)***

Sets of images, ideas and objects that, while retaining their materiality, adequately express thoughts and emotions.
>
> *–adumbration of T.S*
> *Eliot's notion of Objective*
> *Correlative*

BARREN WINDS...

Waking

Waking was the hardest part of it
after a night time of troubled dreams
sun patterns on window panes
reveal a silky morning of ordinariness...
Ah
Waking was truly the easiest part of it...
after the play of sun patterns
on broken window panes...

Sunset on broken gongs

Sun has set before apocalypse
on piles of broken gongs
loose strips of decayed hide
fall of chapped drums
Damp earth soaks
the rancid sweat from horn-blowers
and players with rattling shells
> *King makers and village*
> *chieftains (behind the clan head)*
> *cower under the threatening*
> *fruits of an Ukwa tree*

Father, look at the stampede
among the limpid dances,
the TORNADO lurking on
the edges of the village square...

Day and night

Night pops out tired fingers
to cradle a mangled fetus
conceived at earth's birth-watch

Sun recedes,
angry at the confident strides
of dauntless eclipse,
caught in the asphyxiating trance of
meditative visions
tomorrow gropes, sure the race is on

Today comes tepidly
shedding the suffocating scaffold
of cloying birth
still damp from the fresh showers of season's end

Potent images incarnate fertile dreams,
a distant piper blows
ash-dust off his flute,
wipes his nose and
salutes the birth of inert dawn...

Wilting

Maize seeds rust on their cobs
ant-ridden, they show
pink gums of diseased teeth

Flowers wilt at season's turn
wondering at the unfertilized soil
not far from the homestead

Moist earth welcomes
unripe apples as they fall
from over burdened branches

Stagnant water breeds
festering flies that in turn
plague the pond-maker

Still images radiant with life,
trapped in a certain rapture
of their sad moments
we grin at the rupture within,
vibrant with decay

Now that the pages are turned
see then smudged pictures
from yellowing leaves...

The noise is stilled

The noise is stilled
I answer no more
the calls of music-makers,
your oriki is a soul's dumb echo
a lingering whisper of embattled rattlers

The noise is stilled
sudden silence has returned
amidst discordant sounds
let sudden silence return
for the music makers are no more

Harmattan is the warmest season
when the noise is faintest
January approaches with an *Ijele* thread
Bearing the calm of yuletide

The noise is stilled
for sudden silence reigns

Fire-flies

Out of the past
with mating toad's croak
yet tempered by its cosmic burden
soft as caressing wind on whistling pine

> *If you saw me then*
> *If you saw me then*

I wasn't always like this
panting along time's road
breathless from a moment's hiccup
a virgin was once won in combat
across the slopes of Njaa

> *If you saw me then*
> *Chanting the praises of earth-priests*

(poked fire sends out tiny sparks
sudden light frightens even
…closer for comfort…)

> *If you saw me then*

New masquerades have
taken over the swept Ilo
new priests celebrate forbidden rituals
dissipation empowers restless quests
as strangled innocence flees from the onslaught

(the fire slowly dies to forlorn glows
Retreating shadows converge
Closer, still seeking comfort)

> *If you saw me…*

It was abrupt

the sudden stillness
a death of a kind
as though ravaged by unexpected violation
or still more, a remembered error...

Pale moon lifts over the crouching mountains
Casts blunted shadows here and there...

(poked fire has gone down again)

If you see
the quietude among restless slumberers

In-between

Gentle darkness broods
softly,
incarnating
the fresh smell of damp earth
on the fall of first showers

Pale silvery lights are stilled
now,
before the break of certain dawn
yet under the grip of stale night
like a boa in a wire mesh

Morning peeps timidly through
blanket of scaffolding clouds
sure the time has come
for night to retire

Day soon breaks on damp earth
licking the scent from first showers
darkness is stilled
after the break of confident dawn

Day becomes stale
gripping fresh night in a bear-hug
a pool ripples in the setting light
reflecting the face of tired day
and the half-face of gentle night

Dark offering

A shortlived euphoria
mauled by dark despair
coils, snake-like, in a dusty alley of want

Jubilations are now over,
street corners, pregnant with desolation,
mask the early morning's joyous riots
at the birth of awaited news

City-halls have emptied out
Flatulent men and their bewildered poor
Cousins

Have beat a hasty retreat
to shabby corners of the immense town
only scattered bits of bottles
and broken table legs
speak of a welcome carnival

> *uniformed ants move busily about*
> *wagging fingers at empty shops*
> *muttering some forgotten songs*
> *of their first carnage*

Village squares are silent too
the last echo of the *Ikolo* has long died
down
after the thunderous ululations
wrought by the breathless town-crier's news

Now all is quiet all over the land
seven seasons have passed
(the eight is hiding in the shadows)
since a stillborn euphoria
fell prey to dark despair

> *helmeted ants are still busy in their parade*
> *indifferent to the changed face of the moon*

The chief celebrant is about to go
(only him and the ants hold the stage)
surprised at his clansmen's answer
on the news of seventh season's harvest...

> *the ants still play their shrill flutes*
> *singing victory songs of their fifth coming...*

Gloom

Radiant gloom everywhere, after dissolution
soft lights are playing on barren fields
shadows are now gathering
smothering the quiet wrinkles of fire-flies

exultant eclipse, spread-eagled in descent
mirrors the half-world of grey ash
and another of solemn waste

eager, rides moment's meteor
revealing heaps of split images,

night steals in
rousing the pale face of another time

37 seasons before the tornado

It is written in the book of prophecy...
thirty seasons of agony
seven more to come
before the tornado

Conceived on the threshold of two worlds
devotees of the four barren winds
before the second moon of the sixth season
let loose monsters of the whirlpool
like carrion-eaters, they tore the mangled
flesh of their victims

March of the ants
ushered in the sixth season
who salute the air
with bayonets of flesh
and drank from jugs frothing with gore

Songs of carnage and madness
when clansmen lost their heads
hypnotized by invisible spirits
unleashed mutual slaughter
to mark the passage of three seasons

fertility gods were merciful
to the peace offerings of high-priests
on the gentle prodding of clansmen

Dry river beds became wet
teeming with golden fish
fertility soon brought waste
dragging in an impatient doom
to crown the end of the fifteenth season

The joyous haste of the next season

was slowed by hesitations in the following three
when poisonous seeds started sprouting
ready for harvest

In came the robed gods
who danced for four seasons
granaries were devastated
in the feasting with *Ikolo* sounds
and thousands of talking-drums
the land lay panting
on the grip of foretold dissipation

Soon
the ants were marching everywhere
in broken columns nonetheless
and countless other re-formations
after twenty moons of bitter frenzy
the taste became sour
like saw dust in bruised mouth
or smarting eyes after onion scent

Season of the anointed one
who is the new clan-head
with retinue music-makers
who produce every tune
and molders on clay
who have all the answers
the wise sage is there
so are the thirteen retired wizards
and the enthusiastic umpire
(overseeing unorthodox wrestling)
magicians and fortune-tellers
bring up the rear ranks
for they know season's secrets
one more season will come
to announce the Tornado

The third coming

I
The old King's passage is welcome news
new regents provide but a temporary relief
next season's crowning promises a change
to arrest the hunger in the land
and stifle monsters in their cradle

Leaders of the clan are gathered
(over faintly glowing fires)
for the safe delivery of awaited birth
the master scorer, also called clan-head,
holds the centre stage...

Seven wise wizards stand apart from the rest
attired in brilliant multi-colours
of the major realms,
each incarnating the potency of different lives

No contest it is
just a parley in the clan square
where all may assemble to
test the wisdom of their hearts
and judge the efficacy of their portions

Over burdening loads of immense herbs
enough to ensure the fertility of the young
squeaks from talk-boxes
sufficient to divine the source of the third coming
light-footed flights of embattled town-criers
certain to halt the march of uncaring hunger

Retinue of music-makers
with rattlers, flutes and talking-drums
sing not the panegyrics of brave sons

but the glory of the seven wizards
and their foremost chief priest

And from the clan head
the first proclamation...
All you gathered clansmen
remember the multi-colours of priestly garbs
remember that one alone is your salvation

> *the ball rolls on the soft, greenery pitch*
> *the first dribble is unspectacular*
> *yet breaths are stilled in an anxious moment*

I was there too
watcher from the edges...

In forbidden outskirts of the clan
where outcasts make their home
in the dense forests writhing in desolation
where sojourners are warned of white bodies
in swampy marches festering with diseases
home of those whom the gods have cursed
in village squares where titled elders hold court
and palaces ensconced inside high walls

the wizards cast their rattling cowries
sound their tingle bell
and scan the wide world

...echoes of radiant dreams from the outcasts
...sounds of potent thunders from white bodies
...visions of new dawn from those accursed
...and mocking laughter from titled elders
...and palace chiefs,
...certain in the unchanging face of the sun

the wizards' divination portends danger
secrets should be guarded closely

lest the dim eyes of the damned see clear signs
amulets should not be made common
lest the uninitiated reveal oracular wisdom

Nevertheless, one flees
sulking at a betrayed profession
afraid of the expected stampede

> *the ball is in centre pitch now*
> *dribblers are in head long rush*
> *Maradona is leading the pack*

Hesitant to sound the talking-drum
caught in the trap of differing tongues
frightened of the magic of the outcasts
afraid for a tarnished profession
the six remaining wizards pronounce a cure...

Though different mediums
chant multiple tunes
though the clan land is diverse and wide
and muttering voices thick and dense
our mirrors reflect a clear picture
ugly even to our trained eyes
...echoes of radiant dreams
...sounds of potent thunders
...visions of new dawn
...dominate the centre stage

> *the penalty arc is within sight*
> *the goal-keeper is busy in slumber*
> *Maradona's talent and the Hand of God*
> *proclaim a victory of mocking laughter*
> *and the unchanging face of the tired sun*

From the clan-head the second proclamation ....

Wizards are sometimes there to humour us

their little fees are paid from overflowing granaries
parleys and holding court are provided for
as in the beginning
so be it

The wise old man is happy
truly the assembly is unruly
the shouts acrimonious and unbecoming
with impetuous youth
harassing tested elders
(who have seen two seasons already)
with their clamouring for a new beginning

Truly, it was a trying time
at moments clenched fists and blazing eyes
spoke of lost wits
some moments were sad
with the walk-outs and protests
some moments were tense
with anxious stalemate over
knotty issues of the soul

Yet the wise old man is happy
for the job has been done
weighed down by steaming pots of herbs
and goat skin bags of clay chalk
and potent roots,
he awaits the presence of the clan head...

> *the first half is into dying minutes*
> *dazed defenders are poised*
> *at the onslaught of rushing dribblers*
> *Maradona towers above the rest...*

The clan leaders emerge
(the clan-head is the first to step out)
magicians and fortune-tellers soon follow

to test the offerings
of the wise old man
smug with assurance

I, in the reserve bench
watching from the sidelines...

Two steaming pots are smashed
(there are three altogether)
from the remaining one
(which the old man likes least)
the better herbs are flung out
three of the bags are burnt
(they are five in number)
their ashy clay chalks and roots scattered
prey to rampaging whirlwinds

> *the defender's tackle is feeble*
> *there is stampede at the goal-mouth...*

The sudden spell is broken
a magician hastens to console the old man

And from the clan-head the third proclamation...

The third coming should be delivered
from mouths of oracles and fortune-tellers
clansmen's offerings are tasty
but remember you the weakness of mortals...
the clean-swept *Ilo*
and the feasting at the assembly
came from the harvests
in our overflowing granaries
they are no waste
as in the beginning
so be it

> *Maradona powers home a shot*
> *from the edge of the six yard box*
> *the goal-keeper's outstretched*
> *hands are just too late...*

The umpire is full of unbridled enthusiasm
called fresh to oversee the wrestling
in the newly swept *Ilo*
he is optimistic of a fair contest
truly the beginning was rowdy
given the motley crowd of pretenders
and amateur wrestlers with intemperate energies...

the skinny ones grumbled loudly
terrified at the unbending rules
Soon,
Soon enough, expectant spectators relaxed
full of applause for the contestants
from the thirteen strong villages
bristling with thinly-veiled confidence

> *the second-half is only ten minutes old*
> *expected changes are made at the defence...*

Muted protests were drowned by joyous ululations
when seven contestants were disqualified
for foul-play and inexperience
leaving the centre stage for the dauntless six
truly it is difficult to tell them apart
old patches adorn their new lion-clothes
greasy stains soil some bright spots
their thighs and arms display youthful muscles
on their faces
you are not so sure again
for they reflect the changelessness of toughened hide

Confused about such chameleonic spectacle

Embittered about their unorthodox strategies
the clan-head
(with his magicians and fortune-tellers)
is advised to hold court
for a winner must emerge...

> *the long throw sails over several heads*
> *towards the eighteen-yard box*
> *an attacker weaves his way through spread legs...*

And from the clan-head the fourth proclamation:

The third child
must not be born of broken images
that reflect darkly films of the past
we wanted fresh sons from the fields
and all we got are half-old men
panting along time's road
gripped in a mock-struggle that is no match
the town crier must send for fresh wrestlers
at least two
who will learn the game afresh
under the wise guidance of the magicians
with you the umpire still in the village square...
our granaries are still full
for one more round of wrestling
as in the beginning
so be it

> *a banana shot it is*
> *again from Maradona*
> *which takes the goal-keeper unawares...*

I from the sidelines
I marveled at the three goals...

Incantations on the third coming

How many cock crows must a tapper hear
To awaken from slumber
Walk along dew-drenched paths
And tap frothy wines from slippery trees

How many goals must insipient dribblers score
Before harassed defenders perfect their trap

How many still-births do mothers need
To know the repeated callings of Ogbanje

A tipsy wife is her husband's joy
In the warmth of the matrimonial bed

Careless guardians of the homestead
Should not blame stealthy thieves
Luring fowls away with perforated grain sacs

The first coming was between two worlds
The second was conceived in despair

The third portends evil
Writhing in the mocking laughter of a tired sun

Carefully, carefully look at the thickening horizon
And the dry cough of a midday thunder
And feel if sizzling rain

Will not turn into run away deluge
Gather, therefore, all the homestead utensils
Leave not the cooking pots and earthenware jugs
For I am frightened of the coming flood

DELUGE...

Prophecy

Wind moans off the bay of an unknown bight
At sunset,
Then dawn broke
Reflecting ripples in a stagnant water
Thereafter
In thirty-seven seasons' time
There will be tornado in the land

Season of the deluge

I
Thirty-sixth season of the prophecy
One more will roll by unnoticed
Then
There will be sudden flights from the land
Into distant swirling seas

I heard the oracle's voice again:
In the valleys will be blood
Across the plains rotten carcasses
Forgotten in the sudden flight

> *fire on the mountain*
> *run, run, run...*

The flames will lick into all corners
laying bare their putrid waste
columns of marching ants
will perish in the conflagration

The Third Coming
was into its second moon
when a defender's tackle
brought down a dribbler's rush
in a fair play, not a foul charge

Spectators are coming into central pitch
cheering the awaited reversal
sideliners are caught in rapturous huggings
for once are the traps well sprung

I the participant
I led the throng...

> *twinkle, twinkle larger stars*
> *I now know why you shine your light...*

Ripples are now waves
the water is no longer stagnant
the Tornado is around the edges
laying snares for the anointed one
who is also called the clan-head

Again the voice of the oracle:
hangmen will strangle on their noose
the clan-head will leave the throne
when the last season comes
music-makers will also flee
followed by moulders on clay

The wise sage is now senile
the seven wizards are on forced leave
the optimistic umpire is alarmed at season's turn...

Embattled magicians and fortune-tellers
hold court in a hidden hut
wondering at the strange events
perfecting plans to halt the deluge...

> *the attack is mounted from the right flank*
> *the scissors kick is simply dazzling*
> *but it sails over the bar...*

Earth's fingers are no longer tired
cradling a healthy fetus
delivered safe at birth-watch

Returnees are no longer safe
like outsiders who are gone
they too will leave the homestead

Raiders from the sea
and scavengers from the sand

for two thousand seasons
you have fed
the land is now secure
in the hands of the home tenders
Day and night in combat
ceaseless in apocryphal contest
the breath of one will be stilled
and it won't be that of day
for day will be like...

> *Dick Tiger, remember your left hook*

It wasn't my voice you heard
clansmen
that also came from the gods.

Incantations on the deluge

Thirty-six seasons of agony
And one more to go
Evil ones will write their obituaries
Having plundered the clan
And despoiled the granaries
They await the censure of death-throes
The only promise we can give
Masquerades are made human
When their hidden spirit are exorcised
Oracles know this
This too now is our knowledge

Early tappers tap frothy wine
After dousing pestering bees with water
The same for the alert home tender
Awaiting creeping, stealthy thieves
With their perforated grain sacs
The thickening horizon
Brings lighting flashes
And with them welcome thunder

The First Two Comings
Were innocent nightmares
The Third is already crippled at birth
When the Thirty-seventh season comes
Homestead utensils are safely inside
With them the earthenware jugs
Re-built granaries are now locked
Hurrah then for the coming Deluge
It too will signal the approach of Tornado

Hangmen also die

Hangmen with bloodied noose
beware the trap of time
brave though you are
remember the storm in street corners
chameleon is made weak
when its colours rust

> *horn-blowers are paid magicians*
> *even they may serve as*
> *your undertaker at season's turn*

Uniformed spirits of the realm
bold though you are
remember the robed gods
who were once powerful

> *music-makers are also wise*
> *they too will leave at*
> *season's end*

Skeletons can rattle
animating bones that frighten rockets
its taste will be your hemlock

> *praise-singers are also human*
> *they too will chant a different tune*
> *at the coming of Tornado-bearing Deluge*

Courageous warriors in trenches
the smell of blood is everywhere
fighters though you are
remember the blood you sell
it too can be your end

*image-makers work with clay
they too will mold you in
fragments at season's turn*

The participant

The wild cat's call
rouses roosting hens
from their bed of soft branches

> I the spectator
> I have heard it all

Heard the stealthy creep
through slimy undergrowths
and muted squawks
in night's bated silence

> I the watcher
> I have seen it all

Seen the glowing embers
in dark green eyes
and the neck darting of trapped roosters
scanning the pressing darkness
that holds a death song

I the participant
I have felt it all
locked in combat over time
certain that the call is stilled
that dawn may find them safe

Lingerer on life's dim edges
Watcher hesitant to plunge
I the participant will rather dive...

Where will you be?

Where will you be
when feathery rays of a new sun
give birth to a wide-eyed dawn
or when cascading flood
bring to land our drifting sails?

Where will you stand
when waves upon waves
of spiraling water tear
the denuded shores of barren land
probing with lapping touches
that still the mermaid's song?

How will you feel
when forgotten armies in fields
and rusty hands in smithies
suddenly overrun the fortress of Aguda
sending out wild cries of **kwecha**
that echo across seven mountains?

How will you know
when angry twitches of prodigal lighting
radiating waste and darkness
in a sultry twilight
give way to a noon-day tornado
that sounds with a thousand trumpet calls
animating a forgotten promise?

Torn white shroud of an abandoned temple
let in red embers of fire-flies
light as the touch of an arrow brand

Where will you be
when a world runs its muffled course

and like a yolk breaks for the
sighting of a pink-eyed chick?

Past and present

The song has gone round the circle
the choral leader has paused for breath
actors are ready
For the stage is set

The light is subdued
spectators are anxious with bated breath
for the promised enactment
inside the dome-shaped hut

A casual exchange it was
between the well-fed chief
and the lean and hungry way-farer
the loss is no more than a loss
for the women are still fertile

A long thin line of marchers
across warm deserts
and hundreds of friendly seas
the cruel marks are not so cruel
for truly they are baptismal scars

The rider pauses on his saddle
reins in the stallion
and wonders at the silence
a noonday sun pours
showers of blinding rays

The sudden whispers cease
for the rider is unwelcome
a single shot it was
just a sudden single shot
surely it was one that fell,
just one

the others may learn

The prodigals are back
in shapes and colours we cannot tell
their tune is shallow
like the cry of the evil bird
no more the pains of living cities
but the joys of terrible forests
for the returnees are no different

Outsiders have left the homestead
but their music echoes linger
the pumpkins they starved
are killed by our clansmen

In foundries far and wide flung
in barren fields of wheat
in earth bowels and oil-rigs
in shanties, grim and gaunt,
in schools where knowledge has fled,
barricades are erected
for the homesteads must be saved...

It was from a corner
only from a corner
of the dome-shaped hut
that the shouts began,
soon,
soon enough
it was everywhere
a chant: for the homesteads must be saved...

Troika feast

Solitary cactus in desert dunes
baobab at drought's time
and obeche in swamp waste
are troika feast of human gnomes
in platters of shaven skulls

Great minds are gathered
in a forlorn arena
with cowry shells and tingle bells

White robed gods
mingle with easy patter
and hooded figures dance a solemn
welcome
scanning the cruel sky
for a sign or a word

On the outer edges
...only on the outer edges
dazed minions huddle in a bemused gaze
for the rattle of the first shell
and the tingle of miracle bells

Spirit mediums in human garbs
show a dusty film in broken images,
in fragments
sharp and pointed
nonetheless fragments
of frightened oracles
predicting the disembodiment of
desert sand and drought time
of swamp waste and marshland

Broken chants are taken up

from the edges
of cactus dance and baobab sway
of obeche's song in solitary echo

Suddenly
suddenly in sharp gusts
hurricane storm in a maddening haze
leaves a wake of desolation
of cowry shells and tingle bells
of robed figures and spirit mediums

Columns of ants
scuttled back, unable to poison the air
with their shrill whistles
triumphant deluge marches on
proclaiming the end of troika feast

Judgement day

Assembled armaments are on display
in front of the sun-lit square
dane guns mounted on poles
stand solemn sentinel

Awaited guests have just climbed the Okwolo
ready for a hurried inspection
smoking thatch balls
tossed by millions of calloused hands
stir a stampede among village elders

Pandemonium among the uniformed ants
turns into tattered retreat
broken columns form a shield
around the figure of the anointed one
(whose eclipse was foretold by prophecy)
a stray arrow was dead on mark
dark-blood wrapper speak of another dusk

As ants cower in a thousand disorderly flight
in a fire started by a wrathful farmer
over the incessant raids on his poultry
the rout was complete
leaving only the hulking skeleton
of broken spears
the ungainly carcasses of dane guns
and the dusty eagle feather of the
 anointed one
beside his abandoned prostrate body

Initiation

Warm sand cleanses birth sweat
from the new-comer's body
foretelling the bond with mother earth
the old departs with a shot
that the new one may not be born deformed
ash dusts and disused utensils
litter distant forests
in a forlorn heap
chants are passed in circles
in village squares and swept arenas

> *who peeps at me?*
> *at this dark hour*
> *shaganshaga....*

Potent charms and amulets of shrine-worshipers
forestall visitations of envious spirits
led by their chief, Ekwensu

Ritual feasts of the coming season
are passed over evil doers
who sing only yesterday's songs
pebble game in village square
and fresh mound around life's tree
speak of solemn rites
of a virgin journey

The mocking hoots of the cursed owl
and the fretful darts of *Ishirikpam*
carrying the breath of a dying season
are stilled by sacred vigilance

Initiation time is here now
witches are hounded off

together with baleful wizards
that the toddler may yet live
to bring sweet songs to a re-born world

Youth hood is turbulent season
agitated consciousness, free floating
prey to hidden sickness of the old
hasten then merciful medicine-men
that divine oracle may yet guide our steps
against the march of buried past

Now that the new song is learned
now that toddling child intercepts manhood
bring therefore guns and machetes
that he may protect the new song

The march of tornado

I
The air is thick with the smell of blood
as fresh as the scent of misty dawn
vultures are perched on undulating
branches
craning their necks for a better view

The noise of battle is dinful
in the tornado-clad valleys
the air is perfumed with chants
of this and that
merchants are wielders of spears
and customers, carcass tramplers

A new covenant is born
out of the ashes of the old
Okigbo uttered: mother, mother unbind me
 let this be my last testament ...
he spoke in a hurry
for cabinets cannot catch fire
when forests are free of timbers
nor hell for parliament
when the assembly has not begun

> *the songs are no more laments*
> *with swords out of their scabbards*
> *the songs are longer dirges*
> *when the ants are routed in a war*

II
The sojourners have just set out
across tempestuous seas
into the thirty-seventh water

they cannot be back
nor covered with debts
when the battle is still raging and
the casualties many, and uncounted

There are feces all over the Third Child
its cot is rich with acrid smell
whose cloying warmth pervades the air

The Third Child is prostrate on the floor
its fingers clutching at infertile shadows
the Third Child has been trampled upon
in the ferocious battle
in the shadow of the valley of death

> *madmen become specialists*
> *with the ascendancy of lunacy*
> *madmen hold centre stage*
> *(after the exit of the clan head)*
> *when sane people are few*

III
Cousins, look at the times we live in
and shudder at the pain of birth
I was once a spectator
on the fringes of existence
(if you recall)
I too was a watcher on life's dim edges
(that you also know)
participant about to leap
beware of the swirling waters...

I see fishes of all sizes
remember the ancient saying:
big fish from little fish flesh grows
those who are at war today

and those gorging on sumptuous dishes
beware the march of Tornado
its emblem is signed on muddy walls

The clan has become a market place
(there is much bustle and hassle)
the clan has become a poisonous elm
(its bark is pointed spikes)
peep carefully into the forlorn horizon
and watch the drizzling run of water
soon to become a deluge

> merchants are sharing money
> to buy the conscience of the land
> customers are busily munching
> the remnants of their souls

IV

Again, I remember the prophecy
and the oracle's voice
the thirty-sixth season is yet to pass
and now the Tornado is around
oracles do not tell lies
events only hasten their wish

The Clan-head is now jittery
for eighty-four moons
poking combustible embers of
flames which have become effervescent
before the ashes are impotent
the Tornado would have come

Dribblers are no longer dazzling
in their rush across guarded goal-mouths
sizzling shots are deflected
by the pointed headers of alert defenders
goal-getters are now on retreat

after suffering numerous reverses
> *a brighter sun will come to the clan*
> *across several seas*
> *a new light is beginning to shine*
> *after the break of confident dawn*

V
The four barren winds
are up in war again
against one another
the people are red with fury
when the wind moaned off
the bay of a known Bight
at sunshine

There are killings everywhere
painters brush faces of walls
with thick coagulating gore
vultures have left the branches
for the riverbed of blood

Merchants are killed one after another
by dissatisfied customers
at the dangerous turn of trade
music-makers have their drums smashed
by dancers unsure of their tunes

Tornado has come to the clan
before the thirty-seventh season is up
Tornado has settled among the people
Rousing them to war

> *laments have become eulogies*
> *with the birth of Tornado*
> *dirge-makers have fled the scene*
> *with their songs of sorrow*

VI

I saw the shaven heads of the wizards
and the impotent phallus of the umpire
displayed on market stalls
the clan-head's arms are broken
in the rout of the uniformed ants
the clan-head's legs are smashed
when the ants were forced to leave

I heard a voice out of darkness:
dreams turn into nightmares
in restless repose
dreams turn into death
when the soul departs the body

Our dreams have become their nightmares
their nightmares our hope
our dreams are free-floating
with the approach of Deluge
announced by intrepid Tornado

> *the game is now over*
> *there is calm in the clan*
> *the game is now over*
> *with the onset of Tornado*

Tornado sequences

How long ago was it
when the land lay prostrate
famished by the terror of hunger
how long ago was it
when implacable wizards
foretold the Third coming

How long ago was it
when the oracles saw the Tornado
and before then
the march of the barren winds

In the depths of a shrine
shrouded by hanging foliages
in the inner chambers of the gods
scented by sacred ointments
new diviners are crouching low
impatient with eagerness:
when the ants were routed
and the merchants forced to leave
when the dribblers were halted
by customers who are now goal-tenders
the Tornado is certain of a welcome stay
the conception between two worlds
and the second idiocy
heralded the Third coming
wallowing in tragic fate

Now that tappers tap their wine
and the clan is made safe
now that sober wives
abort indecent act
at the approach of dawn

bring down all the trumpets
and horns long lying fallow
for a new song is passed round
among the joyous celebrants
a new music is being made
in a new village square
drums are no longer chapped
after rotten hide
drums are no longer broken
by the haste of uncaring hands
lamentations are only heard in the border
in the midst of the fleeing ants
dirges are sung in horizons
among the routed merchants
tornado has settled after thickening clouds
there is also deluge in the land
and with them too welcome thunder

OTHER VISIONS...

Seven kindred spirits

Coiled in a trapped vision
Idoto worshipper with crucifix scars
initiation of a deracinated spirit at
dark waters of turbulent cradle
distanced from enchanting limits
then come thunder
announcing town-crier with oracular voice

Myth-maker
World apart writhes in desolation
carrying a certain burden of creation
welcome shuttle 'crypting' many visions
gentle tides hide hidden burdens to
awaken the man who would have died

Early torments of assaulted ego
Africa, our Africa sequestered
in Agbo dancer's tragic incomprehension
the casualties are many
in wars long forgotten
welcome state of the nation
in between present and past

An energy in crisis
trapped in a timeless cycle of elucidation
wrenched by liberation dreams
admonishment full of incantations
dauntless one, now the Fourth though alive

Image-maker, singer in village squares
the market day is here
the anguish of oppressed clansmen
is captured in subtle cadences

ride on, kindred spirit
for earth's eye
reveals a moon full of songs

The travelers are ready,
dressed for battle
no more the labourer's song
nor dreams of power
rather
come voices of tornado
to break down stone walls

Delta oracle, minstrel,
labyrinths are not so crooked
when hidden paths are divined
child of emotions, conceived in turbulence
like the traveler and the village singer
we await more eulogies for the people

Shadows flee at bright light
(for V)

You are the soft glow
around the milky edges of the rising sun
warmer of icicles,
silken,
fresh as undiluted dawn
harbingering laughter in my heart

> *the dews are suddenly dry*
> *on meeting the dazzle in your eyes*

Shadows retreat
shadows flee at bright light
all over you...

You are the sultry moon
like embers of poked fire
radiating dreamy songs in night's silence

> *the damp fogs have lifted*
> *when you showed your face*
> *the damp fogs are no more*
> *when you came in...*

Remember the rapture
of a thousand incessant kisses
remember, the hearts' ardent throb
the infinite wish of a troubadour

The truth in my song
(for V)

Churning mud has settled to the bedrock
leaving clear spring water that
reflects a thousand joyous faces

You are the spring water
after the settling mud
the liquid flame
igniting stillness into life

Now that my wandering is over
now that life wears the toga of sweetness
bring then all the music-makers
to sing her *oriki*

One more thing is left
to sing the truth in my song:
that you are you for being you

A meeting

Instinctive revulsion
felt at a moment's breath
of the inevitable encounter
the diverting path-way
mirage-like, recedes

Not to be bridged by feverish strides
then a brief wait for the inevitable
encounter
sluggish, hesitant steps
yet calm in their determined assuredness
vein-riddled flapping breasts
tattered, dusty clothes and careworn face
sore-ridden toes and bloated limbs
feast for bottle green flies
are regular features of the trade

Not so the eyes,
firmly fixed in their sockets
holding one with a trance-like fixation
speak of the raw nerves
of exhausted consciences

A dropping coin and hasty retreat
tell of things incomprehensible

If it's not the bother
or the platitude of rehearsed thanks
if it's not the fear of depleted means
why then the shamefaced glance
the near stumble in squeaky flight
if it's not the acrid smell
of accumulated dirt

if it's not the rancid breath
from the unwashed mouth
nor the ceaseless buzzing
of unrepentant flies

Why then the urge to hide
as if a dusty mirror
reflects our images in monstrous forms

Rupture

Images of broken dreams
fractured at resolution point
Sisyphus-like on cliff edge
Prometheus unbinds ropes of thorn
and binds to fingers of steel

Patterns of shattered hopes
across two strange moons
when darkness gently grips awakening
dawn
lulling emergent light
into a welter of forlorn gloom

The beginning begets a tragic end
meteor-like
incarnating Hughes' raison
melting in an absurd sun
not that we didn't fight
hooded beasts
stealthily deforming a carefully
woven web
we fought all of failures horrors
and tried to manacle despair
yet,
like a chase around a wall
beginning incarnates end
end incarnating the futility of beginning

Kraftgriots
Also in the series (POETRY) *continued*

Joe Ushie: *A Reign of Locusts* (2004)
Paulina Mabayoje: *The Colours of Sunset* (2004)
Segun Adekoya: *Guinea Bites and Sahel Blues* (2004)
Ebi Yeibo: *Maiden Lines* (2004)
Barine Ngaage: *Rhythms of Crisis* (2004)
Funso Aiyejina: *I,The Supreme & Other Poems* (2004)
'Lere Oladitan: *Boolekaja: Lagos Poems 1* (2005)
Seyi Adigun: *Bard on the Shore* (2005)
Famous Dakolo: *A Letter to Flora* (2005)
Olawale Durojaiye: *An African Night* (2005)
G. 'Ebinyo Ogbowei: *let the honey run & other poems* (2005)
Joe Ushie: *Popular Stand & Other Poems* (2005)
Gbemisola Adeoti: *Naked Soles* (2005)
Aj. Dagga Tolar: *This Country is not a Poem* (2005)
Tunde Adeniran: *Labyrinthine Ways* (2006)
Sophia Obi: *Tears in a Basket* (2006)
Tonyo Biriabebe: *Undercurrents* (2006)
Ademola O. Dasylva: *Songs of Odamolugbe* (2006), winner, 2006 ANA/Cadbury poetry prize
George Ehusani: *Flames of Truth* (2006)
Abubakar Gimba: *This Land of Ours* (2006)
G. 'Ebinyo Ogbowei: *the heedless ballot box* (2006)
Hyginus Ekwuazi: *Love Apart* (2006), winner, 2007 ANA/NDDC Gabriel Okara poetry prize and winner, 2007 ANA/Cadbury poetry prize
Abubakar Gimba: *Inner Rumblings* (2006)
Albert Otto: *Letters from the Earth* (2007)
Aj. Dagga Tolar: *Darkwaters Drunkard* (2007)
Idris Okpanachi: *The Eaters of the Living* (2007), winner, 2008 ANA/Cadbury poetry prize
Tubal-Cain: *Mystery in Our Stream* (2007), winner, 2006 ANA/NDDC Gabriel Okara poetry prize
John Iwuh: *Ashes & Daydreams* (2007)
Sola Owonibi: *Chants to the Ancestors* (2007)
Adewale Aderinale: *The Authentic* (2007)
Ebi Yeibo: *The Forbidden Tongue* (2007)
Doutimi Kpakiama: *Salute to our Mangrove Giants* (2008)
Halima M. Usman: *Spellbound* (2008)
Hyginus Ekwuazi: *Dawn Into Moonlight: All Around Me Dawning* (2008), winner, 2008 ANA/NDDC Gabriel Okara poetry prize
Ismail Bala Garba & Abdullahi Ismaila (eds.): *Pyramids: An Anthology of Poems from Northern Nigeria* (2008)
Denja Abdullahi: *Abuja Nunyi (This is Abuja)* (2008)
Japhet Adeneye: *Poems for Teenagers* (2008)
Seyi Hodonu: *A Tale of Two in Time (Letters to Susan)* (2008)

Ibukun Babarinde: *Running Splash of Rust and Gold* (2008)
Chris Ngozi Nkoro: *Trails of a Distance* (2008)
Tunde Adeniran: *Beyond Finalities* (2008)
Abba Abdulkareem: *A Bard's Balderdash* (2008)
Ifeanyi D. Ogbonnaya: *... And Pigs Shall Become House Cleaners* (2008)
Ebinyo Ogbowei: *the town crier's song* (2009)
Ebinyo Ogbowei: *song of a dying river* (2009)
Sophia Obi-Apoko: *Floating Snags* (2009)
Akachi Adimora-Ezeigbo: *Heart Songs* (2009), winner, 2009 ANA/Cadbury poetry prize
Hyginus Ekwuazi: *The Monkey's Eyes* (2009)
Seyi Adigun: *Prayer for the Mwalimu* (2009)
Faith A. Brown: *Endless Season* (2009)
B.M. Dzukogi: *Midnight Lamp* (2009)
B.M. Dzukogi: *These Last Tears* (2009)
Chimezie Ezechukwu: *The Nightingale* (2009)
Ummi Kaltume Abdullahi: *Tiny Fingers* (2009)
Ismaila Bala & Ahmed Maiwada (eds.): *Fireflies: An Anthology of New Nigerian Poetry* (2009)
Eugenia Abu: *Don't Look at Me Like That* (2009)
Data Osa Don-Pedro: *You Are Gold and Other Poems* (2009)
Sam Omatseye: *Mandela's Bones and Other Poems* (2009)
Sam Omatseye: *Dear Baby Ramatu* (2009)
C.O. Iyimoga: *Fragments in the Air* (2010)
Bose Ayeni-Tsevende: *Streams* (2010)
Seyi Hodonu: *Songs from My Mother's Heart (2010),* winner ANA/NDDC Gabriel Okara poetry prize, 2010
Akachi Adimora-Ezeigbo: *Waiting for Dawn* (2010)
Hyginus Ekwuazi: *That Other Country* (2010), winner, ANA/Cadbury poetry prize, 2010
Emmanuel Frank-Opigo: *Masks and Facades* (2010)
Tosin Otitoju: *Comrade* (2010)
Arnold Udoka: *Poems Across Borders* (2010)
Arnold Udoka: *The Gods Are So Silent & Other Poems* (2010)
Abubakar Othman: *The Passions of Cupid* (2010)
Okinba Launko: *Dream-Seeker on Divining Chain* (2010)
'kufre ekanem: *the ant eaters* (2010)
McNezer Fasehun: *Ever Had a Dear Sister* (2010)
Baba S. Umar: *A Portrait of My People* (2010)
Gimba Kakanda: *Safari Pants* (2010)
Sam Omatseye: *Lion Wind & Other Poems* (2011)
Ify Omalicha: *Now that Dreams are Born* (2011)
Karo Okokoh: *Souls of a Troubadour* (2011)
Ada Onyebuenyi, Chris Ngozi Nkoro, Ebere Chukwu (eds): *Uto Nka: An Anthology of Literature for Fresh Voices* (2011)
Mabel Osakwe: *Desert Songs of Bloom* (2011)
Pious Okoro: *Vultures of Fortune & Other Poems* (2011)
Godwin Yina: *Clouds of Sorrows* (2011)

Nnimmo Bassey: *I Will Not Dance to Your Beat* (2011)
Denja Abdullahi: *A Thousand Years of Thirst* (2011)
Enoch Ojotisa: *Commoner's Speech* (2011)
Rowland Timi Kpakiama: *Bees and Beetles* (2011)
Niyi Osundare: *Random Blues* (2011)
Lawrence Ogbo Ugwuanyi: *Let Them Not Run* (2011)
Saddiq M. Dzukogi: *Canvas* (2011)
Arnold Udoka: *Running with My Rivers* (2011)
Olusanya Bamidele: *Erased Without a Trace* (2011)
Olufolake Jegede: *Treasure Pods* (2012)
Karo Okokoh: *Songs of a Griot* (2012), winner. ANA/NDDC Gabriel Okara poetry prize, 2012
Musa Idris Okpanachi: *From the Margins of Paradise* (2012)
John Martins Agba: *The Fiend and Other Poems* (2012)
Sunnie Ododo: *Broken Pitchers* (2012)
'Kunmi Adeoti: *Epileptic City* (2012)
Ibiwari Ikiriko: *Oily Tears of the Delta* (2012)
Bala Dalhatu: *Moonlights* (2012)
Karo Okokoh: *Manna for the Mind* (2012)
Chika O. Agbo: *The Fury of the Gods* (2012)
Emmanuel C. S. Ojukwu: *Beneath the Sagging Roof* (2012)
Amirikpa Oyigbenu: *Cascades and Flakes* (2012)
Ebi Yeibo: *Shadows of the Setting Sun* (2012)
Chikaoha Agoha: *Shreds of Thunder* (2012)
Mark Okorie: *Terror Verses* (2012)
Clemmy Igwebike-Ossi: *Daisies in the Desert* (2012)
Idris Amali: *Back Again (At the Foothills of Greed)* (2012)
A.N. Akwanya: *Visitant on Tiptoe* (2012)
Akachi Adimora-Ezeigbo: *Dancing Masks* (2013)
Chinazo-Bertrand Okeomah: *Furnace of Passion* (2013)
g'ebinyŏ ogbowei: *marsh boy and other poems* (2013)
Ifeoma Chinwuba: *African Romance* (2013)
Remi Raji: *Sea of my Mind* (2013)
Francis Odinya: *Never Cry Again in Babylon* (2013)
Khabyr Fasasi: *Tongues of Warning* (2013)
Immanuel Unekwuojo Ogu: *Musings of a Pilgrim* (2013)
J.C.P. Christopher: *Salient Whispers* (2014)
Ebi Yiebo: *The Fourth Masquerade* (2014)
Paul T. Liam: *Saint Sha'ade and other poems* (2014)
Joy Nwiyi: *Burning Bottom* (2014)
R. Adebayo Lawal: *Melodreams* (2014)
R. Adebayo Lawal: *Music of the Muezzin* (2014)
Idris Amali: *Efeega: War of Ants* (2014)
Samuel Onungwe: *Tantrums of a King* (2014)
Abubakar Othman: *Bloodstreams in the Desert* (2014)
rome aboh: *A Torrent of Terror* (2014)